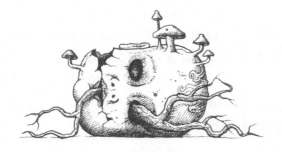

Praise for *The Withering*

"... poetry from a night-blooming blossom ... these poems are a wild view into the mind of a talented young woman, throbbing with incantatory power, and making this reader wonder if she will eventually become the Poet Laureate of the modern Goth subculture."

— **John Shirley**, author of
Wetbones and *Demons*,
from his foreword

"With these verses, Ashley Dioses weaves together the incantatory rhythm of a witch's spell. Luminous language is contorted to reveal dark images, connected to traditional Gothic works and yet not limited by them. The mysterious is entwined with the playful, and the result will lure you to a very beautiful and disturbing place."

— **S. P. Miskowski**, author of
The Worst Is Yet to Come

"The worlds of *The Withering* are bleak, black-white places. The poems of this collection are glimmering, bright-clean bones picked dry, clean and neat. They come from a visceral, bleeding place, and expose a raw, powerful feeling. Guillotines, glitter and even a wry sense of humor, Ashley Dioses' second collection shows just as much talent as the first."

— **S. L. Edwards**, author of
The Death of an Author

Praise for *The Withering*

"*The Withering* by Ashley Dioses is a showcase of rich, gothic delights: an ecstasy of love and life lost. Dioses paints bleak and exotic, lyric hellscapes and lush narratives, often describing eternal, supernatural suffering and vengeance from the inside out. The subtext of so many of these dark, often wrathful poems presents the reader with a plaintive, deeply human question: what am I? Ultimately, the poetic persona empowers herself through an act of self-discovery, answering her own question, exultantly, by addressing the reader (and perhaps Nature itself): 'I am your Monster.'"

— **Jon Padgett**, author of *The Secret of Ventriloquism*
and co-editor-in-chief of *Vastarien: A Literary Journal*

"With *Diary of a Sorceress* Ashley Dioses established her place at the top of the Weird Poetry field. With *The Withering* she shows that she has actually been there for years; like one of the succubi in her poems, lying in wait, ready to dazzle and destroy us. In the modern era, Weird Poetry has rarely been so sublime."

— **Obadiah Baird**, editor of *The Audient Void:
A Journal of Weird Fiction and Dark Fantasy*

Also by Ashley Dioses

Diary of a Sorceress
Darkest Days and Haunted Ways (Forthcoming)
Diary of a Vampyress (Forthcoming)

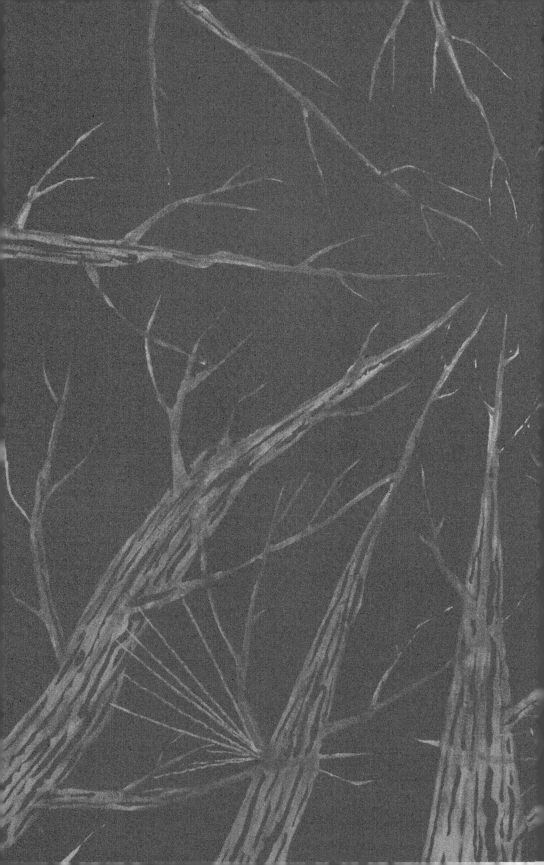

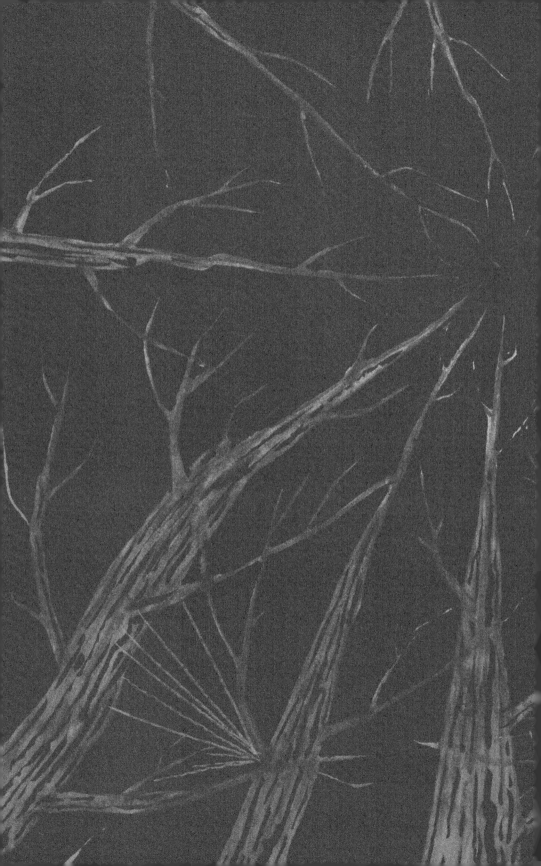

THE WITHERING

ASHLEY DIOSES

FOREWORD BY
JOHN SHIRLEY

ILLUSTRATIONS BY
MUTARTIS BOSWELL

JACKANAPES
PRESS

First Paperback Edition

1 3 5 7 9 8 6 4 2

ISBN: 978-0-578-82360-7

This book is dedicated to the memory of
Terry D. Scheerer

CONTENTS

I. A LUMINOUS DARKNESS

II. PALE RADIANCE

III. NIGHT CRIES

IV. A IS FOR AXE MURDERER

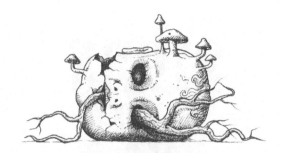

MAJOR ILLUSTRATIONS

SIREN OF SHADOWS

JOHN SHIRLEY

Herein find *The Withering*, poetry from a night-blooming blossom, little more than a bud: a young woman, exploring the dark shadows of her inner world, like a self-made Jungian. These poems are early works by Ashley Dioses, composed when she was in the process of discovering womanhood, together with her identity as a human being, and her curious place in the wide world; she was exploring the mysteries of life and death, guided by fantasy classics and earnest books about magical ritual; prompted by primeval instinct, perhaps transmigratory intimations, and a subculture that whispered of secret wisdom. She was a fan of both dark literature and dark rock'n'roll— so was I too and so I remain—and also of the darkside of classic poetry, like the verses of Edgar Allan Poe. Did she also come upon Lovecraft's book of poetry, *Fungi From Yuggoth*? Did she somehow come upon the mid-century wonders of *A Hornbook for Witches: Poems of Fantasy* by Leah Bodine Drake? Ms. Drake was an esteemed poet, and a descendant of the demonologist Jean Bodin, and Monsieur Bodin (who was more worried about demons than celebratory of them) would have been horrified to read that, according to Ms. Dioses, her poem "I Am the Most Beautiful Angel" "... was originally the second part of two poems which revealed that the angel was Lucifer."

Like many young people, Ms. Dioses was fascinated by horror film and television, and reveals that some of her poems were inspired by these screenings. But while an ordinary youth would have noticed only the horror elements, and taken the whole thing as a cinematic roller coaster ride, Ms. Dioses evidently used them as springboards into contemplation of their deeper (if unconscious) implications. Encounters with two forms of intolerant Christianity seemed to have been scarier to the young Ashley Dioses than her forays into horror and occultism. There are poems in this book which seem subtly concerned about some disapproving deity or parent, as the two can be curiously mingled in one's mind. But with a kind of whispered maniacal glee the poet doggedly continues her course, planning artful homicides; envisioning the taking of human trophies, and generally sending the power of the feminine principle against her enemies. Consider this excerpt from "The Guillotine:"

> I do not care for the blind herd, I still
> Feel that my death will mean nothing to them.
> I wish they'd feel the crisp, refreshing chill,
> And see that they are each a treasured gem.
> Beneath their fully fleshed and weakened form,
> They are divinity, a revelation
> That contravened upon their structured norm,
> Which also led me unto my damnation.

Or this bit from "A Soul of Filth:"

A soul of filth, this is the plane,
The icy voice said through the grin.
We do great things for the insane.
Then monsters rose, besmirched by sin.

(We note that one of Ms. Dioses' favorite rock bands is the memorably named Cradle of Filth.) Over and over the poems assert a determined inner power, a defiance, a willingness to test the numinous energies of the moon goddess against the scorching torches of those who would burn witches at the stake.

Several themes interweave the book; there is, for example, the theme of the serial killer, from an adolescent delight in shocking with paeans to cannibalism to the more sophisticated "A Haunting Sensation Part 2." A hinted-at eroticism in vampiric encounters materializes in several of these works. Deceptive sorcerers; deceived lovers; a decision to turn to dark entities for a kind of strange redemption; a resigned and undaunted alienation.

Ms. Dioses never roams far from her storytelling instincts; she's also a writer of dark fantasy tales and in "Karmic Repercussion" she begins a complete tale told in verse with lines that, but for the rhyme, could open a short story:

Awoken by abrupt sense overload,
He thought he was conjured for a righteous cause.
Exiled to rest forever by cracked laws,
A jolt reminded him of his old code.

There is a certain stylistic tension between some of the poems here, though all are in some sense in the same slashed-open vein; but that tension is also a thread, a connection. Take the first poem in the volume, and try it out as song lyrics. It is without doubt musical in its phraseology, its rhythm—and it's a modern music, though there are reverberations of the bardic. The second poem is more like a rubbing on 19th century romantic versification; has a touch of Swinburne about it. Here, Ms. Dioses' inner classic poet is trying to burst out; she makes quite a number of appearances in the book.

In her later poems, post *The Withering*, Ms. Dioses comes to compositional adulthood. But these poems are a wild view into the mind of a talented young woman, throbbing with incantatory power, and making this reader wonder if she will eventually become the Poet Laureate of the modern Goth subculture. Certainly, we see her finding her voice and singing the wicked songs of the siren of shadows...

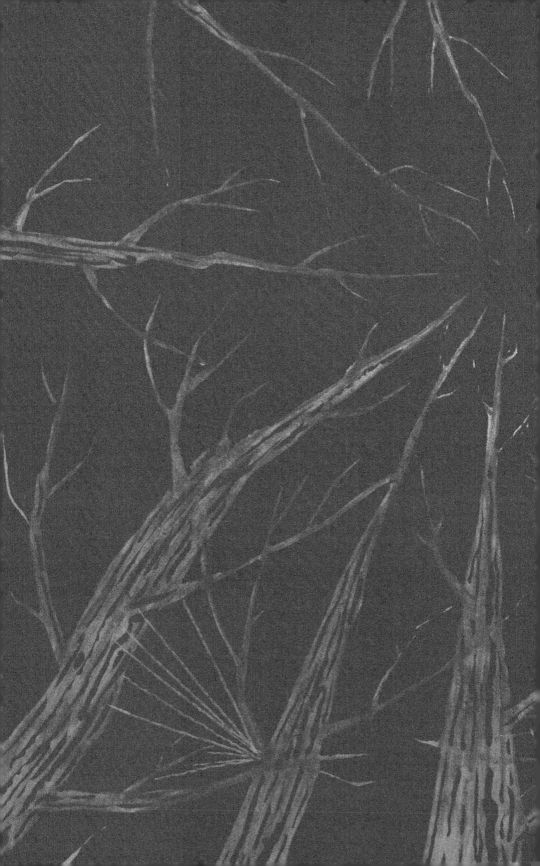

I

A LUMINOUS DARKNESS

A Luminous Darkness

In the white lustrous beams of light,
The shadows quickly fall away.
They scatter, frantically in flight
Once the abysmal night betrays.
They sometimes linger in the shade,
But they will never suffer death.
They sometimes watch but will not fade,
Though fragile as a single breath.
Excitedly, they lie in wait
For the round moon above to rise.
Unquenched, their thirst they need to sate
With brightened moonbeams from the skies.
The cosmic flames of starlight litter
The vast expanses of the sky.
The speckled heavens glint like glitter,
Yet there are shadows who still shy.
And when the yawning moon shall conquer,
Just like a glimmering white flame,
The shadows they will flow and wander,
While putting murderers to shame.
So luminous a darkness, night
Engulfs the caked red earth, and yet
Reflections of the moon's bright light
Beckon to shadows without threat.

Cobwebs

At night, the shining stars illume the lifeless twine,
And glisten radiantly as crystal rain-drops capture
The tempest, which assaults the silk with harshest rapture.
And yet the silk endures in shelter of the pine.

Her eight legs dance across the beaded threads of silk,
Towards the wrapped and bound-up corpse she once called groom.
She tastes his body's splendors, savoring his doom.
Delicious delicacies are taken from his ilk.

The dawn approaches and she rushes to retreat.
Without regret, she leaves her husband's body cold.
She'd bound him up and left him, a display to hold
As trophy, till she can entrap another treat.

Light Fades in Her Dark Embrace

She rises with the frigid night,
And slumbers when the darkness fades.
She searches for a tasty bite,
And lingers in the foggy glade.

Her hungry yellow eyes both shine
With the abysmal star-lit sky;
She patiently awaits to dine
On prey that, in her grasp, will die.

A life draws near, she catches scent
Of blood that thunders from small chests.
Her icy spirit is hell-bent
On catching prey in their warm nests.

The tiny mice squirm underground
In terror of the serpent's grip.
She does not even make a sound
As she devours them, nose to tip.

The light fades in her dark embrace
As life surrenders their last breath.
The cold arrives with horrid grace,
And leaves behind the kiss of Death.

Plague's Wake

The barren land was still,
And not a sound was made.
The plague brought death with skill,
And it refused to fade.

No single wolf did howl.
No raven called its caw.
No cat's desirous yowl.
No humans at the saw.

At first it took a town,
And conquered next a city.
The plague would not back down,
And felt no trace of pity.

What followed in its wake,
Those left would not forget—
The lives the plague did take,
And its persistent threat.

It left a single mark
At first, with just one touch.
So soon the eyes turned dark,
Then they were in Death's clutch.

It swallowed up hoarse screams,
Then all were without life.
Now light no longer gleams
In eyes touched by Death's knife.

The mark was just the start;
A kiss then, on pale lips.
It traveled to the heart,
And left it a cold crypt.

Life Decayed

The icy hands that steal
The life-force out of you
Have now upheld their deal;
You join the Reaper's queue.

The darkness stole your hope,
And all your dreams were shattered.
Nothing could help you cope;
Your life was then left tattered.

Your silky, softened skin
Had turned so green and sour.
You let the darkness in,
So slowly, hour by hour.

For you, it is too late.
Alone, you have been picked.
It was left up to Fate;
Your clock its last has ticked.

Your time has just run out;
What else is left to do
Than leave without a doubt
That this was right on cue?

At last, the Reaper came
As you lay there afraid.
The ravens sought to claim
Your corpse, a life decayed.

Obliterate

All kingdoms come and fade,
Through yellow sands of time.
They pass into the shade,
Neglecting reason, rhyme.

The castles waste away,
And kings will meet their end.
Their enemies will pay,
With nothing to defend.

The stones erode away,
And tales evaporate.
All memories decay,
The years obliterate.

Unveiled Star

The nighttime sky unveiled a recent star
To brightly shine amidst their vibrant kind.
Though they are gone they never will be far,
For in your heart they dwell for you to find.

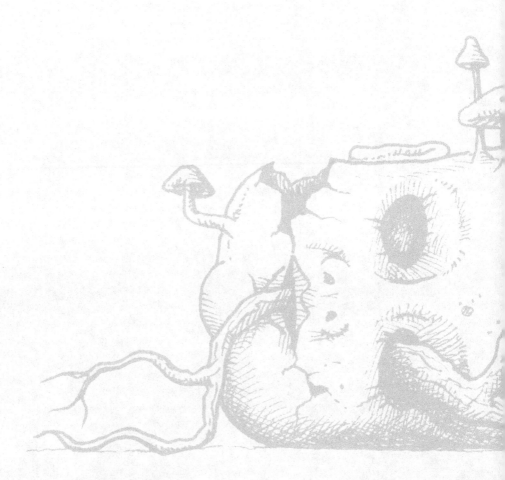

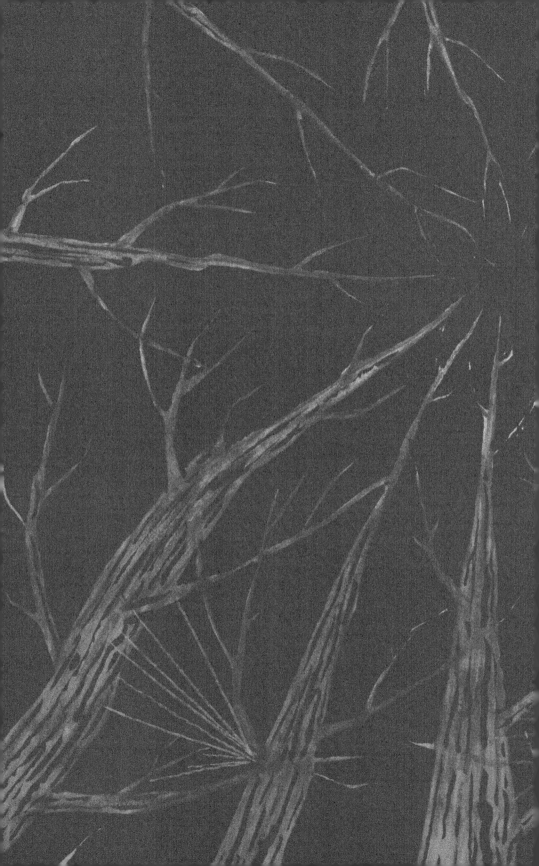

II

PALE
RADIANCE

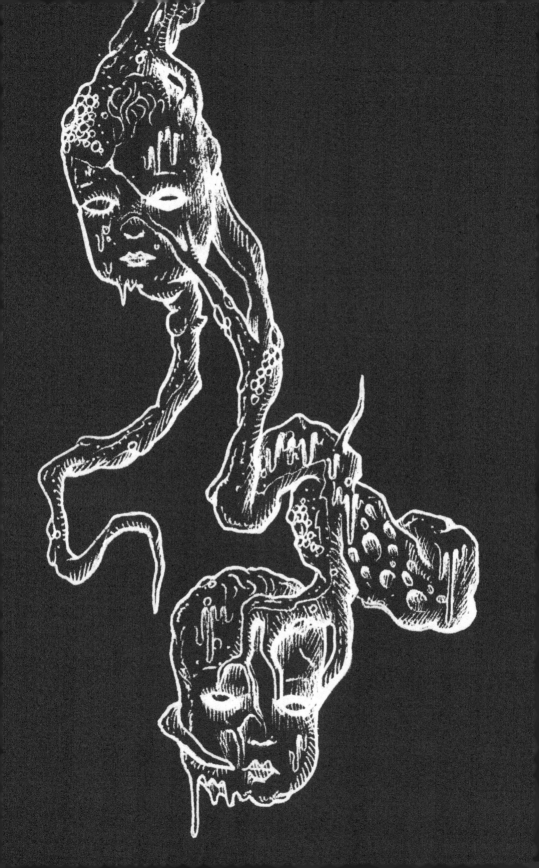

A Lust for Blood

Hot electricity was all he lastly felt.
No matter how hot though, that heart would still not melt.
He did not scream, nor gush, nor moan, nor even twitch;
Instead the room echoed with laughter in the pitch.

He knew he would return to this eternal world
From out the womb of Hell where he was lastly hurled.
He fell to Hell's dark depths, yet landed with such grace.
As he arose, he had the Devil yet to face.

He stood before the Enemy of Heaven's God.
He knelt and bowed his head, and with the slightest nod,
The Devil ranked him as a general of the dead.
He rose and wielded all the powers of doom and dread.

He signed his name inside the blackened book and won
A life of vengeance, and he now would have his fun.
That soul of his was such a tiny price to pay
To murder several victims in his deadly play.

The Damned deserved a leader and he was the one,
For he inflicted torments worse than any gun.
He garnered such a thirst that never could be quenched,
And soon would leave this world entirely blood-drenched.

He felt the surge of power through his muscles flow,
While through the universe all time began to slow.
He was no longer human, but was now a sire
Above the ghouls and even the ancient vampire.

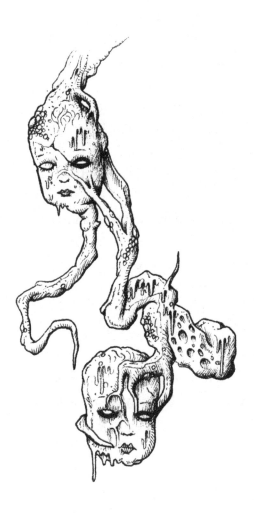

THE WITHERING

Quest for the Flesh

Arise at night when sun takes flight;
Awaken with the moon.
A chilling breeze is just a tease
For what is coming soon.

A breath you feel, which makes you squeal,
Still lurks inside your mind.
The nighttime stars have healed your scars
While you are in a bind.

The loss of hope and things you cope
With leave you with a lie.
The path you take will make you shake—
Yet will it let you die?

You grasp your past but that won't last,
For lust infects your core.
Her body chills as her blood spills,
Yet you are craving more.

The quest for flesh, the human mesh,
Ignites your blood-mad slave,
Your eyes alight when she turns white—
You leave her in a grave.

Dead Kings Rise

The murmurs carry through the air,
Demanding fallen kings to rise.
Their souls were blackened with despair,
And drenched in honey-covered lies.

They hungrily consumed the hate,
Empesting all the atmosphere
Of damned and dying realms. They wait
To devastate the far and near.

With strength and power they emerge
With broken, cold, and tattered hearts.
With whispers they provoke the urge
To kill and see all torn to parts.

And yet dead kings who rise again
Shall fall unto the dust once more.
They fall with the ill fates of men
Who did their bidding, starting war.

Into the Dark I Came

Into the dark I came,
A place no eyes can see.
I wait there without shame,
Till life just cannot be.
I'm one with burning stars,
And blackness of the night.
I have erased my scars—
I died without a fight.

Karmic Repercussion

Awoken by abrupt sense overload,
He thought he was conjured for a righteous cause.
Exiled to rest forever by cracked laws,
A jolt reminded him of his old code.

The scent of fresh-dug earth stirred in him first.
So faint, a vision of a time long gone
Of when a sorceress sought a new pawn.
So skilled with words, she spoke a spell well-versed.

Escaping torment from his darkest cell,
Her brilliant ice-blue eyes ensnared his sight.
The darkened sky, bespeckled with starlight,
Did not attract him once he fled his hell.

With pallid complexion and with trembling skin,
His savior stood so weak in front of him.
She seemed so fragile and her face was grim.
She was a stranger, yet she felt like kin.

The shovel in her hand held her full weight,
Which quickly made him wonder as to how
She just unearthed his ancient corpse and vow....
He knew then, long ago, she once was great.

She was the Sorceress, darkly divine.
An incarnation weakened she was wrought,
For once she left her blackened heart to rot;
Her fiendish ways had led to her decline.

To aid in her advancement, she sought how
To cure her karmic repercussion by
Retaking her enchantments, which still lie
Inside her servant, yet he would not bow.

"Save me," was the command, not the request,
Uttered from out her delicate vocal cords.
He quickly thought of slicing them with swords;
His mind so quickly darkened in protest.

Her magic hold upon him was so thin,
Despite the great and ancient soul she'd shown.
Her body matched that of a wretched crone;
A price to pay for such a wicked sin.

Vehemence hit him and with all his might
He broke her ever-long enchanted curse.
Now death would come, though it would not be worse
Than still obeying her without a fight.

He grabbed his sword and ran it through her chest.
Her piercing screams brought him the sweetest bliss.
He then awaited the Grim Reaper's kiss
When He arrived to lay them both to rest.

Like A Fixed Star

If you can find my tarnished soul
Then you can have my heart.
As soon as I again am whole,
We'll never be apart.

Beware of what you blindly seek,
My ancient heart is cold.
My favor is not for the weak,
For once, my soul was sold.

The djinn who lurk in desert sands
Have placed their eyes on you.
To end up in their hungry hands
Would mean your life is through.

You sought me for so very long,
So greedy for my favor;
So lured by my ancient song,
A melody you savor.

O Goddess great, I hear you say,
A daemoness to some;
My price is very steep to pay—
Yet still you surely come.

Forever hidden and afar,
I lay betrayed and broken,
Bewitching like a fixed gold star,
Bedimmed by curses spoken.

The ancient spells and binding runes
Entrapped my heart and soul.
Interment under desert dunes
Had taken quite a toll.

Once sweet and pure as silk I was
To my unfaithful love.
His curse was not without its flaws—
I called for help above.

My call was heard by one nearby;
A djinn came to my aid.
He said that death I would defy;
My pain, my soul, would fade.

When I agreed to give my soul,
He grinned and laughed at me.
He promised I would waken whole—
But not to set me free!

Grim legends from the aeons past
Enticed a few to seek me.
My luring grave-song would not last—
Yet they would chant obsequy.

I feel your deeply hidden weakness—
You need a mighty queen
To cure your life's unending bleakness;
Your woes are now unseen.

I soon became so cruel and cold
From years of solitude.
My perfect pureness would not hold
In silent desuetude.

I am not soft, I am not sweet,
I am not innocent—
I'm filled with darkness and deceit
That fosters discontent.

Yet you in turn can be rewarded
If you return my soul;
If my hard heart is dearly hoarded,
You'll fill that gaping hole.

My ancient patience has grown thin;
My tolerance is weak;
Erase your stupid painted grin—
My soul is hard to seek!

The darkest magic locked me here,
Yet queen's blood lies within.
My lover's mistress was a seer
Who poisoned me to win.

An unknown plot to rule the throne
Emerged; I was naïve.
Their evil schemes I should have known—
They plotted to deceive.

Though they are now both cold and dead—
My vengeance still is not.
If my pursuer has not fled,
A lover I have caught.

If my new slave could not destroy
My soul's one daemon keeper,
Then I would do it and enjoy
My present for the Reaper.

If it is truly a success
And my pure soul is fine,
My newest love I will possess—
His heart and soul are mine.

THE WITHERING

Djinn Deceiver

A sorceress grew weak and old,
Her magic was all dry.
A deity's touch, she once was told,
Was needed for that high.

A djinn then came to match her pace,
And asked why she was blue.
She asked him for one last embrace—
Yet with it, he was through.

Hollow King

Asleep, my skeleton lies under shadowed sands,
Beneath the once high kingdom of old fallen stone.
Screams were my company as they usurped my throne,
Entombed me, left me for the scarabs of these lands.

They called me Hollow King while cheering for my fall,
And yet my sorceress intoned a spell for me
To rise again within this world, renewed and free.
I hear her whispers—yet, like a fixed star, she stalls.

Her siren serenades call mortals forth to free
Her from her sunken prison deep in desert sand.
My people killed us both, then buried her and banned
That we be near in death, for fear that she would flee.

One day we shall escape and then retake my place.
Yet until then, I lie in wait with her sweet voice
Echoing through my mind—yet that would be my choice,
For I'm in Heaven and she still has Hell to face.

Xyre

Down blackest depths of the abyss,
I fell from light.
Despairing, I could not dismiss
That I lost sight.

The darkness softly shrouded me,
For it seemed trite
That it would grasp with certain glee
And wrap so tight.

From far beyond the shadows' reach,
A star-filled night
Did hold the sorcerer that would teach
Me of great heights.

He sought afar for one so fair;
Not only bright,
But with dark taste to add some flair
To what she writes.

His lulling poetry of love
He'd soon recite
To capture then his treasured dove
Without a fight.

The sorcerer, great Xyre, freed me—
My own true knight!—
From my forlorn melancholy,
And set things right.

In whose own world do we exist?
With all my might
His charms I just cannot resist.
Maybe...not quite...

But would I even want to leave?
Though he may fright,
I still no longer need to grieve
Or soon take flight.

The Sorceress's Lament

The towering walls I built were only meant
To save myself from love's most tiresome songs.
My melodies so soon became laments
When my soft heartstrings for his tune did long.

Too deeply falling is a fault I bear,
For love, to me, is bound not by life's trifles.
Yet even so, as strong a love he shares,
Within him now, his feelings he would stifle.

The talk of magic, love and journeys, fights—
I thought that he was like the knights of old!
The high walls all but fell for such a sight—
But I then learned they were just stories told.

The fairytales wrought from my few ideals
Left me so sad they were not realistic.
Knights gave no chase if it did not appeal
To schedules tightly made and so simplistic.

And yet I always had believed in them.
I traveled past far lands and sought out quests.
I have healed wounds with magic whence they stem.
The love I saved from sadness was a test.

And now I fight the weakness gnawing me.
Such heavy blows my heart has surely taken,
And though my love for him not once did flee—
My heart was rattled and my soul was shaken.

He was no knight in armor, but a bard;
For stories he revealed he had the mind.
I was the knight at arms who would get charred—
I have the true heart that he needs to find.

The Prideful Scribe

Within deep dark unwavering strongholds
Thoughts incandescent burn with depths untold.
Xyre sits, his mind forever in upheaval,
And there are rumors, there is talk of evil.
I scoff at this, for I alone can see
Inside the sorcerer there's love for me.
I am a prideful creature, I've no shame;
These vices conjure walls and we're to blame.
Yet in the prideful scribe it hides too deep—
But where one's blocked, the other still may leap.
Forbidding ramparts may forever leer,
But if he does not break them, them I'll clear.
His rarest runes and lore he may still scrawl—
Perhaps one day those towering walls will fall.

Crimson Swirls

The light in my blue eyes has faded
To wide abysses darkly shaded.
A thousand years has left me cold,
And this unceasing pain untold
Has driven me beyond insane—
I wonder if I live in vain.
A past few hundred long-dead lovers
Were skinned and made to serve as covers
That ever keep me company
And lend me an epiphany.
With one last breath, I take their life,
And with one prick of my prized knife,
Their red, red blood drips in the fine
Clear crimson swirls which I divine.

All Hallows' Awakening

At once, I fall into a sleep;
The agony is dire and deep.
My heart and soul are sparrow-black
With ice invading every crack.

I lie beneath the hallowed ground,
Where Hallows' Even spells abound.
Only the humans I despise
Have powers that can make me rise.

At first I hear a human hum;
Then scents of smoke, of myrrh, of rum,
Pervade my senses from atop
My coffin, which lifts up, then drops.

I hear their chanting clearer now,
Their necromantic spell and vow.
They call to me to set me free,
And suddenly my eyes can see.

The hollows of my sockets stare
At necromancers standing there.
The humans know of what was done,
Yet I'm the one to have the fun.

"Arise," a man demands of me,
And I obey this loathsome flea.
My ancient bones begin to stand;
They smirk as spellcraft goes as planned.

A crimson liquid then is poured
Into a cup; I stand there, bored.
"Drink now." The man hands off the drink.
I mutter at its golden brink.

Yet as I savor its rich taste,
A curse awaits them in their haste
To summon me. Their lives I need
To live again, to kill, to feed.

A strange sensation burns inside,
And fills my veins with blood and pride.
My flesh reforms, again I thrive,
As I am newly made alive!

My laughter I can hardly still
At their misfortunate cheap thrill.
I close my eyes and utter spells
Acquired from hidden crimson hells.

The necromancers' bodies chill
As they discover all my skill
In sorceries of old, and they
All start to die from rank decay.

They all begin to drop like stones;
Their every breath revives my bones.
Our places now have made a trade;
Their bodies soon will all but fade.

I drink until the final drop,
Still waiting for their hearts to stop.
Their bodies lie this autumn night
As I arise to former height.

They each receive what they deserve;
Now Hell is where they ever serve.
I shall descend upon this land,
Their wicked grimoire in my hand.

Pale Radiance

Inside an open casket,
Inside a grave unearthed,
Her head lies in a basket,
Her stolen soul rebirthed.

The witch who lies inside it,
That drained, decaying shell,
In death could not abide it—
She'd rather be in Hell.

The dust would surely cover
Her corpse like delicate lace.
None hear the drum above her
Of her cold heart's lost race.

A pale radiance purely
Illuminates the night.
Beneath the soil, surely,
Her fragrance haunts the site.

A pallid moon hangs lowly
Over daisy-covered glades.
Her skeleton sighs slowly—
A final breath that fades.

Paper Doll Displays

I am forever trapped in a display
With curling tresses and a bright bouquet.
My dress is trimmed, I'm meant to play so well,
A paper doll amid this stand-stilled Hell.
We wait in silence with our plastered smiles,
All lined up straight like soldiers down the aisles.
And when the darkness falls we turn our heads
To our Creator, whom we'll rip to shreds.

A Soul of Filth

He anxiously lies trembling there
With angels, daemons, fae alike.
Their piercing gazes are nightmares
To see; He wonders if they'll strike.

They all conspire amongst each other,
And yet they do not move their lips.
A stillness settles, then it smothers;
Awareness ceases and pain slips.

Then sorrow swells in angel eyes,
And daemon faces darken smiles.
The angels say their sad goodbyes,
While daemons take him to his trials.

Down on his knees, his head is bowed.
Afraid, his face is forced to see
Bedeviled eyes through a dark shroud
Of blackened fire, a smoky sea.

"A soul of filth, this is the plane,"
The icy voice said through the grin.
"We do great things for the insane."
Then monsters rose, besmirched by sin.

The plane was filled with wails and cries.
That mortal soon became a ghoul.
His soul was sold for only lies.
He serves beneath the Devil's rule.

An Angel's Fall from Grace

The solemn passage of a death remains
The same for each and all immortal souls.
Yet destinations change across the planes
When some are pure and some are singed by coals.

Today and aeons past and future, I
Set out to guide them to unholy ground.
Each angel bears their fall from grace from high
Above where those unblemished are all crowned.

Tears of Eternity

I cried out when the lightning struck
And Heaven left me far behind.
I've lost the fight and all my luck;
Forever now, I am confined.

My wings have darkened and are shattered,
I cannot die with such a shame.
The graying feathers all have scattered,
I cannot live with such a fame.

The light is never so forgiving,
And yet the tempting darkness can.
The torment feels it is outliving
My ageless and vampiric span.

I do not know what I'm to do,
I do not know of giving aid.
He said that I will find my cue,
And that it starts with a fair maid.

I walk upon this lonely path
In search of that fair maiden's cry.
I've felt all Heaven's angels' wrath,
And I'm afraid I'll never die.

Eternal life is not, it seems,
Desirable, for they'll take me,
The daemons, and destroy my dreams.
I must be strong to shake them free.

I ran into him once before.
He loomed above me to admire
My beauty. Evil to the core,
His heart was black, his eyes were fire.

I will not weaken in my knees,
Nor cower from his flaming gaze.
I'll stand as tall as all the trees
And match his eyes of fiery haze.

But I can't fight him, that is that.
And even if I tried my best,
The gods alone can smite that rat,
And maybe after I can rest.

At last, I heard the silence break;
It was a shrill, blood-curdling scream.
I ran, for life was now at stake,
And then I saw a vampire's dream.

The woman's blood was everywhere
As she cried out to gain my aid,
And yet I froze, just standing there,
Entranced amid the bloody glade.

My teeth grew long and sharp as her
Heart pounded and her pale cheeks glistened.
Her eyelids dropped, her sight a blur;
Her breaths were slowing as I listened.

If pardon wasn't what I sought,
I would have asked her soul as price.
I'd take it straight to Hell to rot
Amid abysses, fire, and ice.

I don't wish to return to Hell,
Because from there I ran away.
When faced with Heaven, though, I fell,
So now I'll help this special prey.

"I'll cause your suffering to fade,"
I whisper softly in her ear.
I help her from the dampened glade,
Her cuts and pain all disappear.

She looked at me and touched her face,
Then spoke while looking at the soil:
"Again, you still may join our race.
You've passed the test and proven loyal."

I gazed upon her face in shock,
Then gave a faint and weakened smile.
The angels I shall never mock,
But still my heart is foul and vile.

The kill, the blood, I'll surely miss,
But from eternity there fell
My tears at each bought soul, what bliss,
For I forever served in Hell.

Behind Dead Eyes Part 1

She walks down halls of stone
Where she can be alone.
She knows no melodies,
Just life-long tragedies.

Joy has been left behind;
Just pain inflicts her mind.
Hate burns inside her soul,
And leaves a blackened hole.

She always will feel pain,
And lingers on in vain.
She helps innocents' plights,
And constantly stops fights.

She ever walks this Earth
For whatever it's worth.
It does not want her here;
Her purpose is not clear.

She cannot leave this place
Whose past she soon must face.
It's driving her insane,
Tormenting this domain.
Her curse eternal lies
In wait behind dead eyes.

THE WITHERING

Behind Dead Eyes Part 2

She knows all tools that harm,
And every darkest charm.
It's all been done before,
But fools will still make war.

Her watch forever rests
Upon the fools and pests
Who scatter over Earth,
Yet judges not their worth.

Her curse was life forever;
Her foe was very clever.
Once bound for sweetest Heaven,
She now is not forgiven.

She used to search for pardon,
But was denied the Garden.
This world has gone to Hell,
Yet she will help its shell.

Yet as she walks through night
She slays the damned on sight.
She shows them all no favor;
Their blood she loves to savor.
Seraphic corpses lie
All still behind dead eyes.

I Am the Most Beautiful Angel

I welcome you to my domain,
My home where I am king.
My little pets, my sweetest slain,
Come face what Death would bring.

You will forever stay, of course,
You need not ever pray.
Most beautiful, I am the source
Of Venus, none can stray.

O hear my trumpets screech in Hell
As they announce you're here.
I smirk and watch as you each sell
Your souls, held not so dear.

I listen to your pleas and cries
As punishment comes swift.
I watch as hope escapes your eyes—
Your soul is set adrift.

The Entrance

I am the gate, eternal life awaits.
I am the gateway without pain or hate.
I am the way where you will start anew;
A way of life eternal and so true.

Just come through me and I will set you free.
Just come through me and you will truly see
That life with me is life that is divine.
Just enter through my doors; your life is mine.

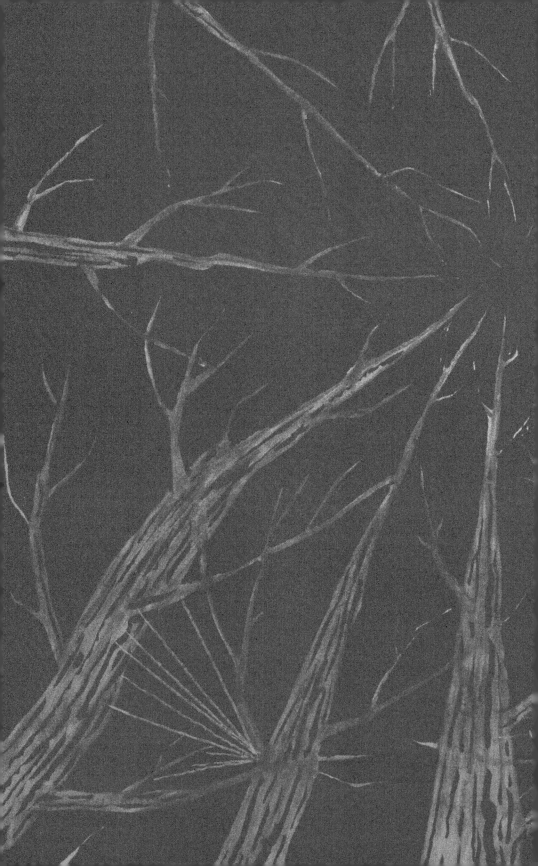

III

NIGHT
CRIES

Twisted Sayings

The fierce unsteady flame
Reflects my thoughts of blame,
Like searing claws that scratch my tainted mind.
The vibrant moonlit sky
And crackling candle's cry
Evokes events I tried to leave behind.

The twisted sayings flood,
And cravings for sweet blood
Arise and I, too late, see what I've done.
My deep subconscious screams,
And no cherubic dreams
Bestow a kiss like lovers in the sun.

The stinging shock invades,
While armies dark parade
Around and I am forced to bend my knees.
I hold my wooden cross,
And pray for all that's lost.
I ask for pardon and ways to appease.

Then manic laughter fills
My soul as the air chills
Me to the bone when voices call behind.
It's steep, the price to pay
For work of my display,
Of blood and flesh, while pardon's hard to find.

I sign in blood the scroll,
And sell to Hell my soul,
A warrior or ever slave in Hell.
The heavens shut me out
For sins, I have no doubt,
And serving under Lucifer's black spell.

This sick infernal curse
Seems only to get worse,
But is it worse than being Satan's slave?
That dreadful fear remembered,
My frozen soul dismembered,
That choice will ever haunt me to my grave.

I bowed unto his will
As shrieks, so very shrill,
Echoed while I succumbed to his demand.
I dropped unto my knees,
Then bowed my head to please,
For after death I'd lead as he had planned.

A transformation takes:
My weakened body shakes
As bones begin to twist and flesh then bleeds.
My teeth are sharp to bite
Beloved necks till white,
And pale to plant my new vampiric seeds.

My prey will then contain
A blackened blood that stains
And taints and chills their very heart and core.
For me there is no end
To all the souls I send,
For Lucifer will always ask for more.

Whispers

When silence creeps and noises cease to grind
Beneath the deepest reaches of the mind,
The voices, many voices, then are heard,
And yet they utter not a single word.

The whispers all start out so soft and fair;
They whisper comforts, yet no one is there.
They purr into your ears and call to you
From out the darkness whence the whispers grew.

Then, like a whirlwind raging in your head,
They fill you up with cruelty, hatred, dread.
The whispers grate through bone into the marrow,
And pass through arteries, so tight and narrow.

Your sanity, for what's left to be found,
Is quickly failing on this battleground.
You try to gouge them out, your stinging eyes,
As whispers say to sever family ties.

The voices call you from beneath your bed,
Then scream and shriek inside your weary head.
They emanate from deep beneath the ground,
And echo off the walls and all around.

The noises, sounds, and growls, this awful din,
Will start to make your whole world swirl and spin.
The whispers have transformed to screams and shouts;
In your own prison there is no way out.

You are imprisoned in your own dark mind;
You can't see past the images that blind.
You see the peoples' faces, oh so vile,
As they transform into daemonic smiles.

Your hair and skin all litter the cold floor;
You try erasing nightmares that you bore.
Your body ceases to protest the sounds,
And whispers still when you lie underground.

Night Cries

Upon this lonesome midnight hour
I pray the moon will wane in power.
I hear, when the pale moon is peaking,
The agony of lost souls shrieking.

It does not matter how they die,
You always hear their sad night cries.
None understand their lasting pain,
Yet they will always cry in vain.

Dreams Forever Will Remain

All of your hopes and all your dreams
Will stay, but aren't what they seem.
Through many years their threads will tatter,
And soon enough the glass will shatter.

The sun and its alluring light
Will vanish soon into the night.
And that's the last that you will see,
For darkness is the only key.

But dreams will never turn on you,
Your hopes have always proven true.
Though you will feel so lost in pain,
Your dreams forever will remain.

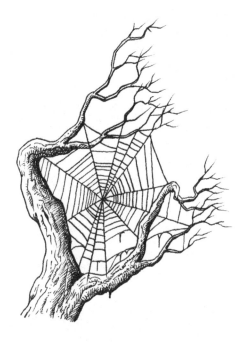

The Sight

Beneath the eerie moon I dream,
Awaking by the sun's bright beam.
But what I see behind closed eyes
Are often torments and dim cries.

Not all my dreams are full of bliss,
For some will end by Death's drear kiss.
So many questions will accrue—
The gift of Sight makes dreams come true.

So when I see these horrid sights
They keep me up on those bleak nights.
Wish not to see what I foresee,
For to be me is not to be.

The Darker Side of Me

The holes in me won't let me see
The light of day.
The pain in me won't let me be;
Inside, I fray.
I feel it all, the rise and fall,
Then drift awhile.
The soul in me is never free,
And turns so vile.
The darker me won't hear my plea,
For I can't stop
The darkness in my depths of sin
Till dead I drop.

Believe Me

Believe me when I say
I've counted all the days
When I was killed inside
By morals tossed aside.

Believe me when I say
I've held my rage at bay—
That all the tears I've spilt
Were from the friendship built.

Believe me when I say
That nothing is okay—
Not hate inside my heart,
Nor pain that tore apart.

Believe me when I say
I've counted all the ways
That I can stop your heart,
And use your corpse for art.

Believe me when I say
I'm pleased to make you pay.
You never will betray—
For this is your last day.

The Picture

You may ignite this frame into gray ashes,
But you will always keep the deepest gashes.
You may destroy the silver-mirrored frame,
But you cannot escape what you became.
You will recall this picture for all time,
For it created a new paradigm.
I give to you this picture for my bliss;
It cannot be erased, save by Death's kiss.
To watch you snap and fall into the ground
Is why to sweetest Hell I'm darkly bound.

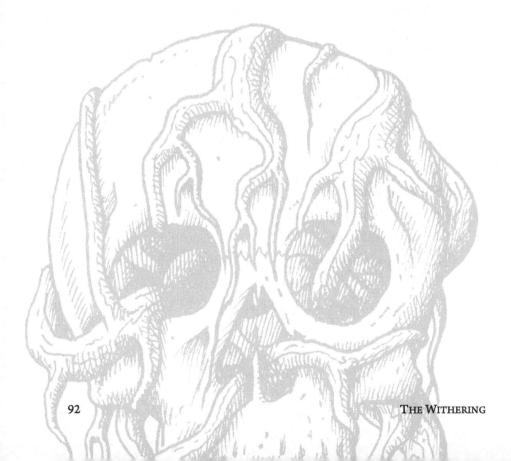

Created

I am the skeleton in your red closet.
The foulest monster under your soft bed.
The evil twin, and what they did to cause it.
The haunting voices in your twisted head.

I am the nightmares in your bright dream-catcher.
The loathsome daemon in your darkest dreams.
The double side of your so riant stature.
The dark heredity sewed in your seams.

I peer inside your deepest, inmost thoughts,
And listen to your voluptuous desires.
I find what you despairingly have sought,
Which burned within, a thousand crackling fires.

I dwell deep down within your wretched soul,
In the abyss of your fragmented mind.
I am as black as the discarded coal,
And the black crawling shadows left behind.

I watch with fiercest hunger as you sleep,
As consciousness so slowly slips away.
I'm always there when silently you weep,
And on the pretty pillows where you pray.

You never even once believed in me.
You have ignored my very mere existence.
But you eventually will have to see
That there is no impenetrable resistance.

I am eternal darkness, that which holds
The vast celestial bodies; moons and stars,
Where the unceasing wishes of all worlds
Are stored inside the mouths of skies afar.

Each woman, man, and even every child
Knows definitely what and who I am.
I am your pain increasingly up-piled.
The curse that surely has severely damned.

I am not just a sole impeding thing;
In this one world of worlds I make up much
Of what daemonic leagues from Hell may bring,
Annihilating souls in one swift clutch.

Your hand is worthless; I do not make deals.
Your gold is nothing; I do not take sides.
A phantom I may seem, yet I am real,
And it will please me to destroy your pride.

I love to hear your mind abruptly snap,
And listen to that lovely sounding break.
I will not tolerate your pleading trap.
I am not something you can really shake.

I am all things gone wrong in your sad life;
All the insanity that infiltrated.
Stabbed in your back, I'm the betraying knife.
Yes, I am everything that you created.

Chartreuse

The blots of blood across the ceiling high
Had suddenly sent minds in motion when
The silent snaps sent brainwaves reeling by,
And feelings numbed to that vile scene of sin.

Two little sisters felt something in sync,
For they were clueless to stains overhead.
They set their backpacks down of pastel pink,
And raced each other upstairs without dread.

Excitedly they entered their play-den,
While shades of scarlet drifted all away.
Their memories were now of mighty men
Who carried out the stench of the decay.

Vivid vermillion changed to chartreuse now,
As the bright tiles bedazzled both their eyes.
The coroner's cold words explained just how
They blocked the gore and saw green tiles and flies.

Then weirder words like "trauma" and like "shock"
Were quickly whispered by all here and there.
The sisters played and still they watched the clock,
Awaiting Mother to come up the stairs.

But Mother would not come to check on them,
For Mother lay there dead and gone and green.
Only chartreuse, the color of her hem,
Remained while strangers sought their Father's scene.

Obstructed visions of some early fights,
Quelled for their own protection, then were stored
Away in both their minds. The truth rewrites
Their brains, it lets the harsh scene be ignored.

Such horror blocked the memory in two
Young sisters of their mother's death; instead
Of bloody red, the chartreuse tiles they see,
And then their mother is no longer dead.

The chartreuse green, it is their sole reminder,
For it will long be etched into their minds.
The waking conscious can do nothing kinder
Than bury memories of many kinds.

The Porcelain Garden

Their eerie blank eyes leer
On gnarled and grassy plains;
Abandoned, left cold pains,
They are objects of fear....

Once cherished and held tight,
The dolls became despised.
Impermanently prized,
The frail dolls suited knights.

The dolls' faux flawless skin,
And iridescent eyes,
Hold shine that never dies,
And everlasting grin.

The girls' innocent wants
Soon turned into desire;
They envied dolls all prior,
Then shattered them with taunts.

The dim Porcelain Garden
Became the dolls' domain—
A sad place to remain
Until their final pardon.

A Haunting Sensation Part 1

You cannot penetrate my precious mind.
I shall not break and you will never find
The truths you seek, for though I bend a bit,
My tongue won't slip no matter how you hit.

My heart is right, my spirit is so strong,
Yet you are weak, your morals all are wrong.
My mouth will never offer what I know;
My secrets stay until I cease to grow.

I'll sit alone in suffering and wait
Until you take my life that's without hate.
I wait amid this dark and teasing silence,
Which will not shatter from my bold defiance.

The pain you mercilessly still inflict
Will strike my flesh, my soul, though you'll not hit—
And yet to live the sorrow and the pain
Haunts me, yet this sensation will not reign.

A Haunting Sensation Part 2

I'll dig in deep because I must unlock
The ever fading ticking of your clock.
I will enjoy it when your psyche breaks—
I'll grasp your secrets, do whatever it takes.

You're growing ever weaker by the moment,
And any time now you will know true torment.
You can't resist my perfect, cruel techniques,
For only Death will still your wailing shrieks.

I shall unlock your thoughts' occulted shrine,
Until those hidden secrets are all mine.
One way or another, you will spill your guts,
With loosened tongue and quite a few spare cuts.

Your agony from one point to a million
Will leave you drifting into red oblivion.
This torturous, psychotic, warped frustration
Is haunting me with such a bleak sensation.

The Creator

I brought you forth from out the black abyss,
And gave you power of the Reaper's kiss.
I tried so soon to take your life away
So your Creator you would not betray.
I was so wrong to not destroy you then,
And you are such a fool, my little wren,
To sing incessantly triumphant songs
Of your escape—it will not be for long.
You cannot fight me—I am your Creator.
I am your mentor—you are but a traitor.

The Monster

You may have made me, but I'm not your slave.
I see that I was living in a cave.
You gave me strength and then you gave me power.
I now defy your reign; it has turned sour.
I now shall rule; I shall take over now.
You are the fool and I will make you bow.
I am your Monster, and you now will pay,
My dear tormentor, for that fateful day.

The Guillotine

The chains enwrap, a serpentine caress,
And sultry breezes lick my shredded skin.
The crowd all shouts, yet I don't hear the stress;
I feel their life-force, just as mine, cut thin.
I do not care for the blind herd, I still
Feel that my death will mean nothing to them.
I wish they'd feel the crisp, refreshing chill,
And see that they are each a treasured gem.
Beneath their fully fleshed and weakened form,
They are divinity, a revelation
That contravened upon their structured norm,
Which also led me unto my damnation.
Or so they think... A chapter now unfolds,
As natural as the wind blows by unseen.
I'm Death's most prized possession, close he holds;
This chapter now awaits the guillotine.

Splinters in My Skin

From the enduring sun to speckled stars,
Each day has brought me closer to the truth.
I'm here to learn how to repair the scars
Accumulated from my lives in youth.

Each life provides a lesson to be learned—
More oft than not I fear I've failed most greatly.
When I fulfill the goal for which I've yearned—
Which is not something that has happened lately—
Ascension will be something I have earned.

My bones are many splinters in my skin;
The spirit of my fleshy form is caged.
It cannot wither though, for it must win—
More lives await ahead before I've aged.

Death Upon Me

Existing scars remind us that the past was real.
The skin upon my form was pierced in far too deep,
So Death has come upon me, and despair I feel
Is from the tears that fall from those few who still weep.

If even I had known I was already dead,
The sudden loss of life would have me no more mourn.
My mind is gone along with my own golden head,
Yet soon I shall awake and once again be born.

Pure evil festers in the eyes of the beholder,
Yet it is not always so clear to know or see.
When he, my killer, looked at me they were much colder;
As hard as rock and cruel as a slow death can be.

What life or death is, even I shall never know.
He, my fair slayer, came and raised his mighty sword,
And when the glinting blade cut swiftly through, down low,
I stared defiant and did not murmur a word.

My life was shortened and though it was absent glory,
My burning soul became a beacon that was greeted
By daemons bent to capture their elusive quarry—
For even with grim Death I never could have cheated.

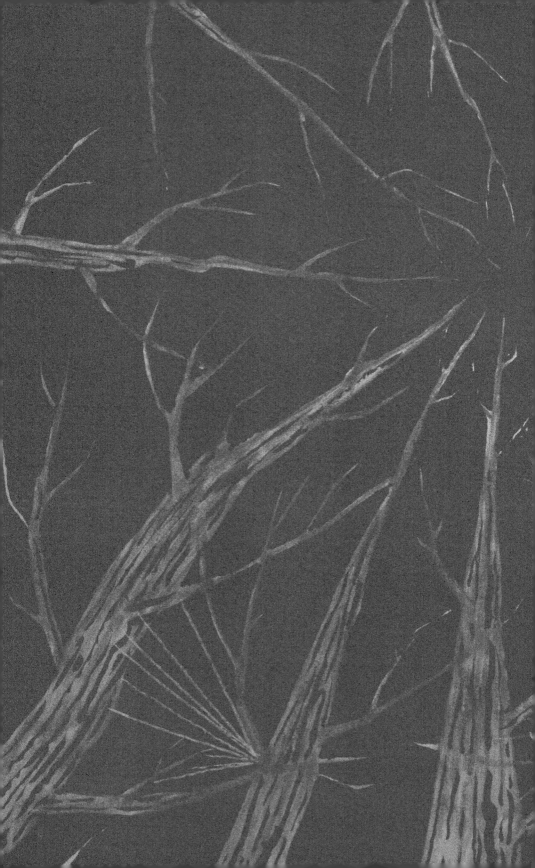

IV

A IS FOR
AXE
MURDERER

Ashley

(an acrostic)

An attitude fit for a fae,
She comes on winter's eve to play.
Her games upon the fields were short,
Left quickly for another sport.
Ere long she sought to feed her spear—
Yes, she would spread despair and fear.

A is for Axe Murderer

A is for axe murderer
Coming down the stairs.
B is for the pools of blood
Smeared with cryptic care.
C is for the cleverness
That I so will need.
D is for the drastic danger
I will need to heed.
E is for electricity—
Eerily, there's none.
F is for my lifelong friends
Who are freshly gone.
G is for the ghastly gore
All throughout my home.
H is for the fiery Hell
Where I hope he roams.
I is for the ill intent
Festering in me.
J is for the utter joy
When I break his knees.
K is for the epic kill
I must execute.
L is for the lasting love—
Now I'm destitute.

M is for the manic monster
Lurking near unseen.
N is for the nasty notes
That have words obscene.
O is for the deep outskirts
Where I'm cursed to live.
P is for my friends in pain,
Acts I can't forgive.
Q is for the urgent quest
For a sharp device.
R is for the sweet revenge
Where I won't play nice.
S is for the blissful screams
Pried from vilest lips.
T is for his streaming tears
Spilled when dermis rips.
U is for the deathly union
We'll together hold.
V is for the few victims
Who will not grow old.
W is for the worms
Burrowing in their brains.
X is for his last x-ray
If life he regains.

Y is for the treasured youth
Lost by their decay.
Z is for his life's last zest
That I tore away.

THE WITHERING

The Surgical Suite

My dearest, you have such messed up heartbeats,
Though it's a joy to play with such sweet treats.
In counting all your ribs through twenty-four,
It is between rib three and five I score!
The flaying of your flesh and breaking bone
Is such a triumph, yet I stand alone.
O shiny scalpels, saws— there's so much skin!
Oh where, oh where, do even I begin?

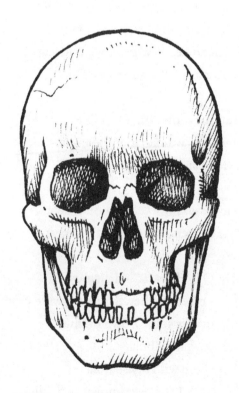

Body Parts

When hunger strikes my gut, it strikes my soul.
A pit infinite, black as any coal,
Yawns wide to gain a taste of weird delights…
"Which body parts?" inquires my favorite vendor,
As he lifts offerings of endless splendor.
My eyeballs gleam with cravings for such bites.

His soul's as blackened as the market shop.
My vendor holds a nicely butchered chop.
It's smooth and skinless, juicy and quite thick.
'Fresh female' reads the glossy paper tag,
Once wrapped up neatly with a rope and gag.
I could not care less if it made some sick.

I marveled at that morsel that was fine;
I knew at once this woman must be mine.
I made the trade and went my merry way.
Cheerleader, band geek, or a great athlete;
My one concern was whether I should heat
Her or, like my revenge, serve cold on trays.

O body parts, O body parts—delicious!
They taste much better when they once were vicious.
I cannot fathom why some frown on this.
I slice her femur to her fibula,
And then I flip flesh with my spatula.
With my first taste, I've never known such bliss…

The Body Shop

A Body's a Body

A body's a body no matter how small,
They slice oh so nicely, no trouble at all.
My pleasure just peaks when their ribbons are soaring;
They all could be buried, but that would be boring.

Sweet Meat

Such delicacies carved with magic signs,
So many myths a body's breadth defines.
Desirous touches of a skin so sweet
Just make me quiver at the sweetened meat.

Bloody Sundae

My rare obscure taste for nocturnal desserts
Includes a red eyeball that nicely converts
To cherry atop my sweet bloody sundae,
Completing my craving for cloying sorbet.

Cannibal

The zealous zombies are quite quaint,
For they crave parts all stained with taint.
A treat of brains will kill the cells,
And cause slow death and putrid smells.
No, I desire a nice soft neck,
A lung or two, and a fine peck.
A strip along the middle of
The back I will soon griddle, love.
A cannibal I have become—
To human taste I say yum, yum!

Strung By a Noose

No razor blades, no wounds that fade,
No smoking gun.
Just give me rope, I have no hope,
And that's no fun.

I'll tie my knot and hang and rot
From the inside.
I'll cut the air and see you there—
Death's a fun ride.

My one last smile shows no denial
That with my breath
I'll curse Man's strife and leave my life,
Then greet my death.

I'll laugh out loud at the full crowd;
My soul will leave
When I'm set loose, strung by a noose,
And none will grieve.

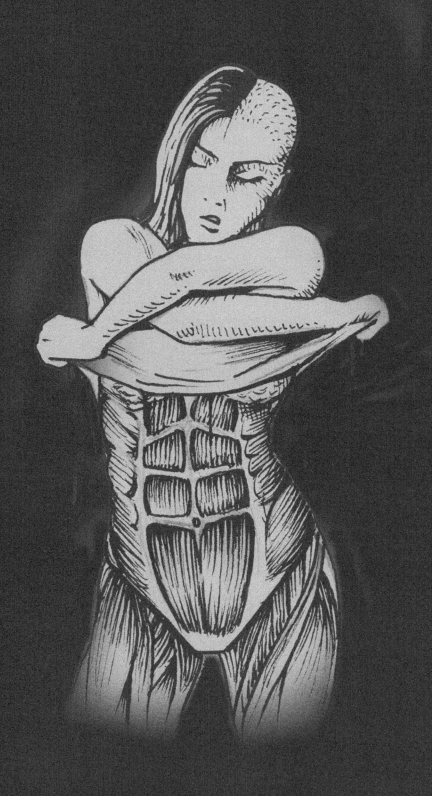

Skinless

There once was a girl
With soft skin of pearl,
With ruby red lips,
And bright bow hair-clips.

She lived in a world
That made her lips curl—
They all looked the same,
No matter what frame.

Rejecting the norm,
Inside her a storm,
She shaved off her hair,
And grinned without care.

Though proud of her move,
It just was to prove
She'd never be them—
For she was a gem.

Then many months later,
A strangeness much greater
Struck deep in her nerves;
Her trendsetter serves.

Nobody had hair,
She gave them all glares.
And instantly thought
Of something not sought.

A notion then struck;
Her skin she would chuck!
With muscles all torn,
A new life reborn.

She strutted in bones;
There were no more clones.
They stood all in fear
When she would draw near.

Entirely skinless,
She felt just so sinless.
She never was sane,
She felt no more pain.

Her sanguine exterior
Just made her much cheerier.
And now without skin,
She held the last grin.

AFTERWORD

I have been writing horror and dark fantastical poetry since the age of twelve. My darker inspirations then included writers, musicians, artists, and movies such as Edgar Allan Poe, The Misfits, Cradle of Filth, Slipknot, Luis Royo, Tim Burton, *The Crow*, *The Prophecy*, and *The Omen* series, among others. *The Withering* is basically the end result of listening to a lot of metal and reading and watching horror.

The Withering contains select poems roughly from the years 2002 to 2014. With much consideration, however, I have decided not to put my poems in chronological order, as might be expected for a collection covering a certain time span. I chose to organize them by themes, which results in a nicer flow. *The Withering* is broken up into four themes: Nature, Supernatural, Psychological, and Physical or Body Horror.

In 2006 and 2007, my high school sophomore math class was the best place to write poetry, and that was where I wrote the majority of *The Withering*. My teacher was a super cool, really laid back guy and provided the best atmosphere for me to focus on my writing and not be distracted by the lessons. I nearly wrote a poem a day during my sophomore year and when I wound up in summer school to retake my math class (naturally), I came up with the title, *The Withering*.

Unfortunately, as my summer school math teacher pointed out (immediately after seeing my 'notes' which consisted of my vision of *The Withering*'s cover), this was my last chance to make up the class, so I reluctantly started to concentrate on math instead of poetry. That was probably for the best.

In my pre-teen and teenage years, I also struggled with religion. My dad was a Catholic and my mom was a Presbyterian. My older brother was baptized as a Presbyterian but because my family didn't attend church, the Presbyterian church would not baptize another child when I was born. I was instead baptized as a Catholic. Neither religion appealed to me.

As a child, I was always interested in stage magic and was a big fan of Harry Houdini. While researching magic one day, I discovered that other magic existed. In 4th grade, we learned about the Salem witch trials for the first time and from then on, my attention turned from stage magic to magick. I learned everything I could about the subject and practices of magick, including various other religions such as Wicca, Asatru, Satanism, and various Pagan spiritualities.

Of course, this did not go over well with my parents. I tried discussing what I was learning and how it wasn't anything evil but to no avail. By the time I was thirteen or fourteen years old, I was deeply conflicted. That conflict took root in many of the themes in *The Withering*. Poems about falling from the light or grace, while trying to push against the darkness, and simultaneously trying to gain back favor, are prevalent throughout the book ("Behind Dead Eyes" and "Tears of Eternity" are examples). It wasn't until I was fifteen or sixteen that I finally broke away from religion. Later poems such as "The Guillotine" and "Splinters in My Skin" began to show the change in my thinking.

From my junior year on my poetry output dwindled and by 2009, I had stopped writing it altogether. My focus had changed to my fantasy novels that I started in middle school.

I finished the first novel by my freshman, or maybe sophomore year, and finished the sequel between my junior and senior year. After high school, I knew I wanted to become a professional writer. Even though I may have been naïve about many things at that age, I wasn't naïve enough to think that I wouldn't need a regular job if I wanted to also become a writer. I went to college and during those years, I decided to check out the publishing world. With the help of my dad, who gifted me my first *Writer's Guidebook*, I searched for submission guidelines in the horror section and tediously wrote down every poem that I thought would fit each submission call. I then sent out poems all over the place.

I hated having my poems sitting around, gathering cobwebs, while I focused on my novels. It felt like all that hard work was being wasted. I wanted the poems to be out in the world—I wanted to put a poetry collection out first, before any eventual publication of my novels. Poetry was my beginning, it was where I started, and is what means the most to me as a writer.

But I had moved on from poetry—or so I thought. Finally, in November 2011, two of my poems were published. Immediately after they were published online, I got an email from another poetry editor praising my work and he invited me to submit poems to the ezine he volunteered for. He convinced me that my talent would be wasted if I didn't continue writing poetry. He encouraged me to start up again and offered to help me hone my skills. So I did, and so I have ever since. That editor's name was K. A. Opperman.

The Withering was planned to be my only poetry collection and my first book. If I had included all my poetry from the years 2002 to 2009, when I temporarily quit, it would contain nearly 90 poems. I have downsized it to contain my best poems produced from the time I started writing poetry again in 2011 up until I started putting *Diary of a Sorceress* together in 2014. *The Withering* contains a few later poems that I felt did not fit with *Diary of a Sorceress*, and contains one poem from 2017 ("Djinn Deceiver") that I felt fit better thematically with the poems in this collection. When I started writing poetry again, the new poems still had the feel of what I wrote like in high school. I didn't notice any style changes until 2014, and most of the poems produced from that year on would appear in *Diary of a Sorceress*.

Though many tortures of the mind and body are displayed herein, I did not wish to torture you with the entirety of my poetic output from my pre-teenage, teenage, and early twenties—much of which could be classified as doggerel. *The Withering* includes the best fifty-five poems from that period, and I think they give an accurate overview of my early style. May these poems entertain and—hopefully—inspire you in a myriad of ways.

—Ashley Dioses

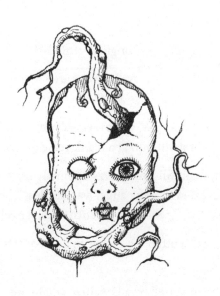

ENDNOTES

1. "Light Fades in Her Dark Embrace" was originally titled "Light Fades from Her Dark Embrace."

2. "Unveiled Star" was originally a eulogy to a friend's sister's guinea pig, Roxy.

3. "A Lust for Blood" was inspired by the movie *Spawn*.

4. "Dead Kings Rise" was originally titled "Amidst the Mist."

5. The title "Hollow King" was taken from a line from the movie *The Scorpion King*.

6. "Xyre" is based on K. A. Opperman's sorcerer character from his collection *The Crimson Tome*.

7. "All Hallows' Awakening" was originally titled "The Sight from Within."

8. The title of "Paper Doll Displays" was inspired by a misunderstood lyric from the song "Through Glass" by Stone Sour.

9. "An Angel's Fall from Grace" was previously titled "Angel's Grace" and was originally my first attempt at a blank verse poem.

10. "I Am the Most Beautiful Angel" was originally the second part of two poems which revealed that the angel was Lucifer. The first poem was titled "I Am Beautiful," with no reference to the angel being Lucifer.

11. "The Entrance" was written for a scene in the sequel to my fantasy book series.

12. "Night Cries" was inspired by a Dreamer's dialogue in the video game *The Elder Scrolls III: Morrowind*.

13. "Dreams Forever Will Remain" was originally titled "They Shall Forever Remain."

14. "The Sight" was the first written record of me experiencing dreams manifesting in reality.

15. "The Picture" was inspired by the song "Unframed" by Ill Nino.

16. "Created" was inspired by the song "Enter Sandman" by Metallica. It was also the first poem of mine that K. A. ever read which prompted him to reach out to me.

17. "Chartreuse" was the first poem I wrote when I started writing poetry again after my long break from it following high school.

18. "The Creator" and "The Monster" were originally a single poem with two parts titled "Tore/Mentor."

19. "The Guillotine" was originally titled "Guillotine Close."

20. "Death Upon Me" was originally titled "Death is Upon Me."

21. "A is for Axe Murderer" was inspired by Edward Gorey's *The Gashlycrumb Tinies: A Very Gorey Alphabet Book*.

22. "The Surgical Suite" was inspired by the Waverly Hills Sanatorium episode in season four of *Ghost Adventures*.

23. "The Body Shop" was originally comprised of the first poem, "A Body's a Body," and titled the same. Terry D. Scheerer, the editor of an ezine called *Horrotica*, suggested I expand on the poem, as it was too short for his liking to publish it.

24. "Skinless" was inspired by an illustration by Stephanie Bowman as well as the poem "Johnny Depp" by Tim Burton.

CHRONOLOGICAL ORDER

1. An Angel's Fall from Grace (2002)
2. The Sight (2002)
3. Ashley (December 2002)
4. Death Upon Me (September 2, 2004)
5. A Lust for Blood (2005)
6. A Soul of Filth (2005)
7. Tears of Eternity (2005)
8. Behind Dead Eyes Part 1 (June 2005)
9. Behind Dead Eyes Part 2 (June 2005)
10. All Hallows' Awakening (2006)
11. Dreams Forever Will Remain (2006)
12. Night Cries (2006)
13. The Picture (2006)
14. Whispers (September 19, 2006)
15. Life Decayed (October 3, 2006)
16. Created (October 17, 2006)
17. Plague's Wake (October 24, 2006)
18. The Creator (October 30, 2006)
19. The Monster (October 30, 2006)
20. Believe Me (November 6, 2006)
21. Cobwebs (November 30, 2006)
22. I Am the Most Beautiful Angel (December 6, 2006)
23. Strung By a Noose (December 19, 2006)
24. Light Fades in Her Dark Embrace (January 8, 2007)
25. Obliterate (January 17, 2007)
26. The Darker Side of Me (January 19, 2007)
27. A Luminous Darkness (January 23, 2007)
28. A Haunting Sensation Part 1 (March 16, 2007)

29. A Haunting Sensation Part 2 (March 16, 2007)

30. Dead Kings Rise (March 23, 2007)

31. Quest for the Flesh (April 5, 2007)

32. Pale Radiance (April 21, 2007)

33. Twisted Sayings (June 21, 2007)

34. The Entrance (September 3, 2007)

35. Chartreuse (December 12, 2011)

36. Like a Fixed Star (January 5, 2012)

37. Karmic Repercussion (February 13, 2012)

38. A is for Axe Murderer (February 17, 2012)

39. The Surgical Suite (March 19, 2012)

40. The Guillotine (March 23, 2012)

41. Skinless (April 28, 2012)

42. Cannibal (April 30, 2012)

43. Paper Doll Displays (May 9, 2012)

44. Body Parts (May 27, 2012)

45. Crimson Swirls (July 18, 2012)

46. The Body Shop (October 26, 2012)

47. Unveiled Star (October 30, 2012)

48. Xyre (November 10, 2012)

49. Splinters in My Skin (November 23, 2012)

50. The Sorceress's Lament (December 24, 2012)

51. The Prideful Scribe (February 28, 2013)

52. The Porcelain Garden (March 30, 2013)

53. Hollow King (June, 19, 2014)

54. Into the Dark I Came (February 20, 2014)

55. Djinn Deceiver (September 10, 2017)

ACKNOWLEDGEMENTS

"A is for Axe Murderer," *Dark River Press* (Spring 2012)

"All Hallows' Awakening," *Anatomy of Hate* (Alban Lake, Winter 2018)

"Behind Dead Eyes Part 1," *The Phantasmagorical Promenade* (Planet X Publications, 2019)

"Behind Dead Eyes Part 2," *The Phantasmagorical Promenade* (Planet X Publications, 2019)

"Body Parts," *Horrotica* (Fall 2012)

"The Body Shop," *Horrotica* (Winter 2012)

"Cannibal," *Caravans Awry* (Planet X Publications, 2018)

"Chartreuse," The Stray Branch #13 Vol 10 (Spring/Summer 2014)

"Cobwebs," *Weird Fiction Review* #9 (Centipede Press, Winter 2019)

"Created," *The Horror Zine* (Winter 2011)

"Crimson Swirls," *Horrotica* (Fall 2012)

"Djinn Deceiver," *The Stylus Issue Two: Journal of the Strange* (13th Hour Books, Summer 2017)

"Dreams Will Forever Remain," *Blood Moon Rising* Issue 51 (Winter 2014)

"The Guillotine," *Dark River Press* (Spring 2012)

"A Haunting Sensation Part 1," *Dark River Press* (Spring 2012)

"A Haunting Sensation Part 2," *Dark River Press* (Spring 2012)

"Hollow King," *Walk On The Weird Side* ed. Joseph S. Pulver, Sr. (Fall 2017)

"Life Decayed," *Spectral Realms* No. 10 (Hippocampus Press, Summer 2019)

"Light Fades in Her Dark Embrace," *Blood Moon Rising* Issue 51 (Winter 2014)

"Like a Fixed Star," *Eternal Haunted Summer* (Summer 2019)

"A Luminous Darkness," *The Horror Zine Magazine* (Fall-Winter 2012)

"A Lust for Blood," *Dark River Press* (Winter 2012)

"Night Cries," *Dark River Press* (Winter 2012)

"Pale Radiance," *The Horror Zine* (Winter 2011)

"Paper Doll Displays," *The Horror Zine Magazine* (Summer 2014)

"The Picture," *The Horror Zine Magazine* (Fall-Winter 2012)

"Plague's Wake," *Spectral Realms* No. 11 (Hippocampus Press, Summer 2019)

"The Porcelain Garden," *The Horror Zine Magazine* (Summer 2014)

"The Prideful Scribe," *Skelos: The Journal of Weird Fiction and Dark Fantasy* Issue Three (Fall 2017)

"Quest for the Flesh," *The Horror Zine Magazine* (Fall-Winter 2012)

"Skinless," *Horrotica* (Winter 2012)

"The Sorceress's Lament," *Spectral Realms* No. 9 (Hippocampus Press, Summer 2018)

"The Surgical Suite," *Dark River Press* (Spring 2012)

"Twisted Sayings," Weirdbook Issue 49 (Wildside Press, 2022)

"Whispers," Weirdbook Issue 46 (Wildside Press, 2021)

"Xyre," *Skelos: The Journal of Weird Fiction and Dark Fantasy* Issue Two (Spring 2017)

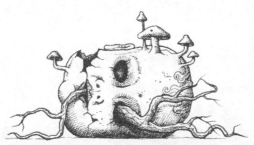

ABOUT THE CONTRIBUTORS

ASHLEY DIOSES is a writer of dark fiction and poetry from southern California. Her debut collection of dark traditional poetry, *Diary of a Sorceress*, was released in 2017 by Hippocampus Press. Her poetry has appeared in *Weird Fiction Review*, *Cemetery Dance Publications, Weirdbook, Black Wings VI: New Tales of Lovecraftian Horror, Vastarien*, and others. Her poem "Cobwebs" was mentioned in Ellen Datlow's *Best Horror of the Year* Volume Twelve. She has also appeared in the *Horror Writers Association Poetry Showcase* in 2016 and 2020 for her poems "Ghoul Mistress" and "Her Heart that Flames Would Not Devour" respectively. She was also a nominee for the 2019 Pushcart Prize. She is an active member in the Horror Writers Association and a member of the Science Fiction Poetry Association. She blogs at fiendlover.blogspot.com.

JOHN SHIRLEY has written dozens of novels, numerous story collections, TV scripts, and screenplays (e.g., *The Crow*). His story collection *Black Butterflies* won the Bram Stoker Award. As a musician, Shirley has fronted his own bands and written lyrics for Blue Öyster Cult and others. His most recent albums are *Spaceship Landing in a Cemetery* and *John Shirley & the Screaming Geezers*. Visit john-shirley.com and screaminggeezers.com.

MUTARTIS BOSWELL is an English artist hailing from the rural West of the UK, where he lives with his partner and two kids while creating his weird and atmospheric worlds. He's worked as an artist for Feral House and Dynatox Ministries, and his illustrations have appeared in various weird fiction publications such as *Spectral Realms, Occult Detective Magazine*, and many others. He also makes underground comix and has been a regular contributor to Satanic Mojo Comix and Dystopian Chronicles. More of his art can be seen at boswellart.blogspot.com and boswellart.bigcartel.com.

JOURNEY ONCE AGAIN TO THE DARKNESS AT SUMMER'S END

"...[K. A. Opperman] is the gifted descendant of poets ranging from Poe to Walter Scott to Robert Burns, all of whom understood that Halloween's deliciously dark mood may be best served by poetry."

—LISA MORTON, author of *Trick or Treat: A History of Halloween*

"All hail The Pumpkin King..." **—DENISE DUMARS**, author of
The Dark Archetype: Exploring the Shadow Side of the Divine

COMING IN LATE 2021
www.JackanapesPress.com
www.facebook.com/Jackanapes-Press

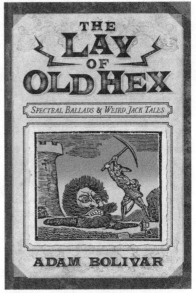

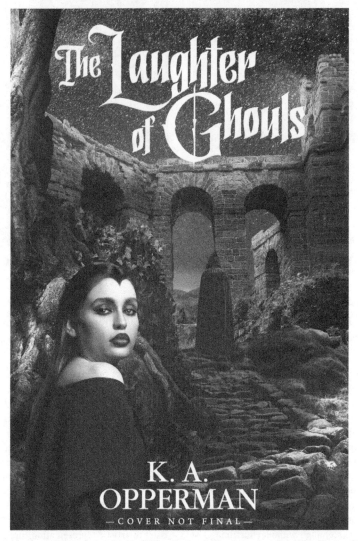 

Made in the USA
Monee, IL
14 December 2020